Snake and Eggs

New Women's Voices Series, No. 168

poems by

Beth Suter

Finishing Line Press
Georgetown, Kentucky

Snake and Eggs

Copyright © 2022 by Beth Suter
ISBN 979-8-88838-044-4 First Edition
All rights reserved under International and Pan-American Copyright Conventions. No part of this book may be reproduced in any manner whatsoever without written permission from the publisher, except in the case of brief quotations embodied in critical articles and reviews.

ACKNOWLEDGMENTS

Special thanks to the editors of the following publications where these poems, some in earlier versions, first appeared:

Birmingham Poetry Review: "The Narrator"
Blue Moon: "Dowsing"
Cider Press Review: "Civilization"
Colorado Review: "Non-Euclidian Geometry Before Breakfast" and "Inheritance"
CutBank: "Field Guide"
DMQ Review: "Untitled"
Flyway: "Cutting Tools" and "Survival Training"
Kestrel: "Gödel's Incompleteness Theorem"
Literary Mama: "For the Daughter I Can't Have"
Little Patuxent Review: "Oil Slick Shine"
Louisiana Literature: "It Could Have Been Anything but It's Moonflowers"
Natural Bridge: "Ode to the Sacramento Valley" and "Relapse"
New American Writing: "Anticipatory Grief"
Poet Lore: "Snake and Eggs"
Potomac Review: "Pieces of the Unbreakable"
Snowy Egret: "Easter Mushroom Hunting"
Tule Review: "I Don't Want to Forget"

Publisher: Leah Huete de Maines
Editor: Christen Kincaid
Cover Art: Still Life with Fruit, Fish, and a Nest, c. 1675 by Abraham Mignon,
 Courtesy National Gallery of Art, Washington
Author Photo: Edward Michael Henn Jr.
Cover Design: Elizabeth Maines McCleavy

Order online: www.finishinglinepress.com
 also available on amazon.com

Author inquiries and mail orders:
Finishing Line Press
PO Box 1626
Georgetown, Kentucky 40324
USA

Table of Contents

It Could Have Been Anything but It's Moonflowers 1

Gödel's Incompleteness Theorem 2

For the Daughter I Can't Have 3

Anticipatory Grief 4

Untitled 5

Easter Mushroom Hunting 6

Snake and Eggs 7

Cutting Tools 8

Oil Slick Shine 9

Field Guide 10

Relapse 12

Ode to Pain 13

Survival Training 14

Civilization 15

Ode to the Sacramento Valley 16

I Don't Want to Forget 17

Dowsing, Early Morning 18

Non-Euclidean Geometry Before Breakfast 19

Apocalypse Birding 20

Pieces of the Unbreakable 21

Inheritance 22

The Narrator 23

for my family
thank you

IT COULD HAVE BEEN ANYTHING BUT IT'S MOONFLOWERS—

standing in for her sleepless shimmer
    my father and I drawn like moths

she planted these nocturnal blossoms
    their wide throats echoing the moon

blue veins under crepe skin, crepe petals—
    I'm tired of writing this lovely dread

this *I wouldn't trade it for anything*
    but the moonflowers return

psychedelic seeds, like peyote,
    you'll get visions and vomit

and under what circumstances
    would a child need to know that—

so what if I didn't moonflower my own child
    part of me wishes I did, or could have

I wonder *what's life without this rapture—*
    it's a lot to ask of a climbing vine

busy being itself, clutching whatever holds it up
    self-seeding year after year like the dream

where my mother pours seeds into her palm
    says *I can't do this anymore*

turns to follow our long-dead cat
    my father and I drawn like moths

GÖDEL'S INCOMPLETENESS THEOREM

*The more I think about language, the more it amazes me
that people ever understand each other at all.*
~Kurt Gödel

there exists a boy
which implies a mother
such that they were one once

(a false statement that's true)

she recurred a self-similar pattern
a human fractal—

the Fibonacci spiral of his ear
like a fern, a fetus unfurling—

too complex to prove
the boy teaches her
no language is absolute

(she thinks of Gödel's mother)

the boy says
*it's a logically derived paradox
that I love*

FOR THE DAUGHTER I CAN'T HAVE

you would have been
another beautiful disaster

my body couldn't bear
another tender scar

I lost my voice
in my son's delivery

now he finds the words I seek

he says *we are foiled
by the mere being of things*

he is my replacement

I dream of you, dandelion girl
what's gone is everywhere

ANTICIPATORY GRIEF

at ninety she doesn't know my name
she knows my smell as her mother's

heads together we speak our first language
hum and hug, point and wonder

patting heads of hydrangeas like babies
everything goes in the mouth

we mimic a *chickadee-dee* singing its own name
I draw the sun, she turns it into a flower

daisy-chain daughter I could never have
it's a hungry nausea, like morning sickness

smell of yeast's last breath raising the dough
I can't eat it away, this bellyache of remaining

UNTITLED

grandma bookmarks
her bible with crow feathers
talks to the sun

born paperless on Chickasaw Creek
she keeps her dark hair short
braids mine like a prayer

suspicious of funeral homes
she says *just wrap me
in a blanket and dig a hole*

pockets full of rocks, she treats
money like a rattlesnake, edible
as long as you cut off the head

EASTER MUSHROOM HUNTING

hungry, we follow the scent
of oak tannin and cave

where just-thawed forest floor
hides meaty, buttery bulbs

the same brown buff
as sun-dappled loam

as if the leaves themselves
became morels

beneath the swell and bulge
of the hollows, they burrow up

into a cold, sheer light
filling us with a wild infusion—

the marrow of the woods

SNAKE AND EGGS

she's no summer petal
between creek-crazy mess
and skin shivering off

        she shatters on, knowing only
        this swallowing whole planet
        a silent vibration, can you feel it—

her boa constrictor childhood
in the jungle of her ribs
muscling the air aside

        there's not enough
        unraveling in the world
        to untie the umbilical

ouroboros, a magic trick
of uncuttable cord
this coiled black hole universe

        like her womb collapsing in
        on itself, an old star
        hotter, heavier

she inherits the snake
story, how it trapped itself
in the chicken coop

        belly too fat with eggs
        how it *fried up good and*
        we never went hungry

CUTTING TOOLS

today the paring knife
        cut me a slice of memory—

my father, sharpening me
        with knife-wielding lessons

he lost his grip
        on a buck knife

made a pinhole for the light
        in my skin—

he once showed me
a catfish heart, still beating
        long after gutting

long after its flesh fed us—

he wanted me to know
        the bloody wonder of it

OIL SLICK SHINE

something smooth to keep in the mind
stillborn calf slick-black in sunlight
the way life spills wide

mussel shell's rainbow oil slick shine
broken blue egg, baby robin blind
something smooth to keep in the mind

orange butterfly sipping a cow's eye
headless copperhead in copper light
the way life spills wide

junkyard's yellow wild mustard riot
train-flattened penny bronze mirror bright
something smooth to keep in the mind

white-booted hound snapping a rabbit's spine
pregnant bluegill mistakenly sliced
the way life spills wide

blackberry-sweetened thorns of briar
ash-blond heartwood of lightning-struck pine
something smooth to keep in the mind
the way life spills wide

FIELD GUIDE

I keep going back to the pelican
in a sparse Oklahoma prairie
the wonder of a creature displaced

I want to tell you about its survival
as if it were something like mine
I want to give you the wordless

with feathers, something light
enough for you to carry
maybe braid into your hair

even if it's from a mockingbird
an escapee from Paradise's ashes
singing like the ones that didn't make it

there ought to be a gospel
in every field guide
a hymnal for those alive and gone

like the white owl
perching on the soft bones
of our drought-stricken birch

wholly itself, no symbol of mine, just
giving you what I've been given
like the sharp-shinned hawk

striking at the feeder—
how the air filled with dove-colored down
hunger's softness

covering the ground like shed petals—
I want to give you the beauty of what's left
like a woman on her knees

overcome by phantom pregnancy
can I tell you a secret?
she named the impossible

fluttering *Phoebe*—
I wish I could give you more
than a prairie girl awed by a seabird

that lone pelican in a split willow
I want to give you its salvation
to tell you it found a way home

or learned to eat catfish from the mud
the child that was me wanted to know
of course I only saw it that once

RELAPSE

in the throat, a clutched dry box
        catches what can't be swallowed

something pulses there
        not as simple as *fear*—

a chokecherry flower's reflex
        to close under cloud—

what can't be said sticks
        where someone grabbed hold

out of 100 abstract nouns
        foreboding sings

like sundown crickets buzzing
        in the required city tree—

decades of peeling skin
        broken limbs in bloom—

another day of petals
        waiting for the chainsaw

ODE TO PAIN

you return with the crickets'
sleepless rubbing

I name you Lucky
my soft-clawed critter

curled in my cesarean scar
you keep me in the moment

like faith you're there
when you're not there

squeezing me breathless
you were at my son's birth

and mine, sting of light
in a newborn's eyes

I can't close my own
to the memory of my sliced self

and the sawing crickets
this night I'm split again

the body a door of dark matter
my life hinged here on you

SURVIVAL TRAINING

grandma says: *if you ain't sure it's edible*
feed it to the dog first

she pickles the abundance of ditches
wild garlic and onion, such relish

gathered summers hoarded
she passes down her dust bowl roots

in her final letter she sent a photo—
the only shot she took that day—

of a winter deer in wild-rose bramble
eating the rusty fruit

she wrote a confession
of hearing it pray

of laying her rifle down, of a hunger
for something besides venison

she mailed the fixings
for her bitter cure-all tea

deer-bitten rose hips
spilling from the envelope

CIVILIZATION

they learn to look both ways
our clever cousins

crows, squirrels, jays, raccoons—
using streetlights to spot what hunts them

choosing a well-fed life
over the forest's hungry beauty

I see this city through their eyes
the security of a well-lit street

nests of shiny rubbish
what do nestlings know of past migrations

it's the grief of great grandmothers
what they traded for our lives

who can blame those first corn-mothers
for clearing ground

for wanting chubby children

ODE TO THE SACRAMENTO VALLEY

I learned to love yellow to live here
your goldfinches and star thistle
your ten kinds of deer grass
the color of my son's fawn hair

from a plane coming home to you
I saw what I missed, your long lines of rivers
and the crops that drink them:
sunflowers and wheat, safflower and corn

drawn to your fields that need harvesting
birds blow in from all directions, people too
I would not have chosen you
just another stop on my parents' migration

but I fell for a valley man with his sunny hair
and drought-tolerant heart
fell for the scent of wild rye baking—
a warmth that leaves me thirsty

I DON'T WANT TO FORGET

winter rain sizzling
in the jacuzzi
your hands under my hips
floating me

*I was the fern, raised
in a hothouse of emotion*

your boxy-brown Volvo
bucket seats too far apart
gearshift and handbrake
as awkward chaperones

*you were the succulent
storing tenderness*

weekends entwined
knowing you in the dark
delicate collarbone
your hip in my hand

*resting in your desert silence
I didn't need an answer*

that first summer
your fuzzy, satyr legs
the smell of sunshine
on your shins

*I chose the dryness
of you*

DOWSING, EARLY MORNING

~for my husband

like a lost stream you fall
        into subterranean stillness

a shifting, rhythmic spring

sometimes I find you—
        a shiver in the forked branch—

you visit me in my sleep

my face pressed into your back
        it's your scent that wakes me

windfall apple wild
        mushroom musk

there are no words
        for what happens next

NON-EUCLIDEAN GEOMETRY BEFORE BREAKFAST

this instant gives itself to me
in this kitchen window
wavy with dishwater and rain

in these droplets that soften the view—
arched trees blurring outside—
in these words that hold the image

in this skillet I'm washing
this film of olive oil that shines
whose olives were rained on once

in this boy who leans into me, saying
our world is curved, that's why
parallel lines bend toward each other

APOCALYPSE BIRDING

> *~Reading* Leaves of Grass *in the PICU*

what would Whitman make of this world ablaze
how my boy can burn like a town named Paradise
fevered, coughing on the ashes of others

> *celebrate every atom, the play of shine and shade*

charcoal clouds of displaced sparrows
flock the hospital grounds
fight over a birdbath's smoke-flavored water

> *hear bravuras of birds, gossip of flames*

they chirp like my son's IV machines
his breath a pop and crackle campfire
of particulate damage that pneumonia loves

> *fly those flights of a fluid and swallowing soul*

like the peregrine falcon that nests
on the hospital's window ledge ten stories up
I teach my chick to feast on what's left

PIECES OF THE UNBREAKABLE

dreams, I didn't want to write about you
maritime museum of dead-eyed sharks

Victorian ropes of hair from lost loved ones
ships made of fingernails

trawling my night's mind, catching
words *pieces of the unbreakable*

they came on a flaked obsidian sea
a carpet of jellyfish and me barefoot

I didn't want to write about you
porthole of water moccasin memories

tacklebox of feathered barbs
how naked I wade in your waters

the ferryman's toll to cross the river
I sleep with a coin in my mouth

INHERITANCE

I must have been filled
       to feel this emptiness

my mother's euphoric light
       a tide surging in, receding—

I could say *bipolar*
       but that would shadow
             the truth—

she lit this sea-cave
       I carry inside

it shelters blind creatures
       who miss the rush—

waves took and returned her
       bioluminescent being—

the sea is not what it carved
       this bright hollow
             in my name

THE NARRATOR

is she tired of making it all shine
showing the reader mercy
using the softest sounds

maybe she'd like to use a pen name like Randy or Richard, spit a hacksaw homesick in short vowels and violent verbs—shit gets ripped, whipped—ditch a buck in pickup truck dust, quote a hard-ass like Bukowski—*love is a dog from hell*—give it that "last call buddy" closing-time sound like she's had too much but won't give up the keys, bark, growl as if she owned the place, as if she'd bite

she opens her mouth to answer
and a mockingbird flies out
singing all the things she's swallowed

Beth Suter grew up in rural Missouri close to grandparents who survived the great depression by gathering wild food. She learned that the forest was both a place to look for beauty and a place to look for lunch. She has had a deep connection with nature ever since and considers herself an ecopoet. She started writing poems as an undergraduate at U.C. Davis while studying Environmental Science and continued writing during her years as a naturalist and teacher.

She started publishing poetry in 2013 and has since appeared in over forty publications including *Colorado Review, New American Writing, Barrow Street, DMQ Review,* and *Birmingham Poetry Review.* She won first place in the Ina Coolbrith Poetry Contest, Nature Category, in 2013 and was chosen as a finalist in the Pat Schneider Poetry Contest in 2015. A 2016 Napa Valley Writers' Conference alumna, she has been twice nominated for a Pushcart Prize and once nominated for a Best of the Net Prize in 2020. She participates widely in workshops and readings both in Davis and at the Sacramento Poetry Center.

You can follow her at *facebook.com/bethfsuter*

www.ingramcontent.com/pod-product-compliance
Lightning Source LLC
Chambersburg PA
CBHW022128090426
42743CB00008B/1054